EMOTIONAL INTELLIGENCE

Table of Contents

Introduction

Congratulations on downloading this eBook on emotional intelligence and in the same breath thank you very much. We all recognize the impact that emotional intelligence has on our world and what role it plays not only in our relationships and day to day activities but also in acting as a determinant in the level of success that we can achieve.

Herein you will find chapters discussing the ins and outs of emotional intelligence. One can finally get to understand the entirety of the word emotional intelligence and learning exactly to what is meant when the phrase comes up. It also seeks to uncover the uses of this intelligence and whether or not it is important in ensuring that we live life successfully and fully. The 360-degree management of one's emotions and how they can harness that power to perform better in their relationships notwithstanding their performance at their work places and career advancement.

There are many aspects of emotional intelligence that have been addressed in this book making it not only a good read for you but also one that is packed with beneficial information advancing your mastery and grasp of the topic. I do recognize that there are a lot of books regarding this matter available, increased gratitude for choosing this one! Each exertion was made to guarantee it is loaded with however much valuable data as could be expected; please appreciate!

Chapter 1: An In-Depth Look Into What Emotional Intelligence Is

Most of us have come into situations where we have heard people throw around the word emotional intelligence often interchanged with the shorthand of EQ and EI. "You should have dealt with that situation with a greater EQ," or "Tom needs to work on his EQ when dealing with people," are phrases that are not new to our everyday lives. And more often than not, we did not take the time to sit and think to ourselves, what exactly is this emotional intelligence that they are talking about. Where does one obtain this emotional intelligence? Is it a cognitive ability that a person is born with or is it something that can be developed? Through this book, we will dive into the deep waters of emotional intelligence, its benefits, how to develop it and how we can use it to successfully manage our relationships.

Emotional intelligence (EQ or EI) is commonly described as the capacity for a person to recognize their personal emotions and those of the people around them. This ability enables them to be able to discern between the different feelings and accurately identify them, and with this knowledge, they are able to tailor their behavior and reactions in managing and adapting to that particular situation increasing the chances of success of that relationship.

The term was first coined in the year 1964 in a paper written by Michael Beldoch. This was only the beginning of what would follow more studies conducted and more papers written on the subject matter. The concept of traditional intelligence types was then introduced in the year 1983 though Howard Gardner's paper, "Frames of mind: The theory of multiple bits of intelligence." This brought to light the concept of multiple bits of intelligence one from involves the capacity to understand other people's emotions and motivations known as interpersonal intelligence and that to understand your own self and what drives you known as intrapersonal intelligence.

The British Mensa magazine were the first movers in publishing the use of the phrase EQ in a 1987 article by Keith Beasley. It however achieved mainstream use and popularity 31 years later in 1995 through the book titled "Emotional Intelligence – Why it can matter more than IQ" written by Daniel Goleman. Daniel Goleman was a world renowned psychologist and science journalist. It was after his book that emotional intelligence became a subject of scientific scrutiny and analysis. This happened in spite of public reports claiming of its beneficial use in daily lives.

There are numerous models through which EI has been described and classified. However, what Goleman first described would at this time be considered as a mixed model. This is drawing features from both the ability EQ model and that of the trait EQ model. In his book, Goleman described emotional intelligence as a variety of characteristics and skills that work in the development and advancement of performance in leadership. Konstantin Vasily Petrides developed the trait model in the year 2001. He claimed that the trait model of emotional intelligence encompasses behavioral inclinations and self-perceived capacities that are in turn dignified through self-reporting. On the other hand, John Mayer and Peter Salovey developed what we now know as the ability model in the year 2004. This model is centered on a person's ability to read and process emotional data and use the information from it to manage their individual social setting.

Studies conducted on the subject matter has then gone to suggest that individuals considered to have higher emotional intelligence have superior mental health, perform better at their tasks and jobs and their skills in leadership have shown to be at a higher level. This is, however, not been quantified in relationships of a casual nature in that these findings can be justified by the people's own intelligence and their personalities rather than their EQ. In his book, Goleman laid claim that EQ contributes to a percentile score of 67 in the undertaking of tasks that determined greater performance in leadership. This had a greater effect when it came to performance in areas that required technical prowess.

Other studies suggested that if the personality traits and the ability of the test subjects were controlled and held constant, EI would not play a significant role in the measuring of both their managerial and leadership performance. These studies claim that general intelligence has a greater correlation when it comes to their leadership performance. However, this has not been without criticism. They have mostly orbited around the debate of whether emotional intelligence can be considered real intelligence and what value does it play against that of IQ in the daily lives of people.

Chapter 2: Importance and Benefits of Having Emotional Intelligence

There are always on going debates on if emotional intelligence is really as important to life's successes and everyday living as its biggest proponents claim it to be. Some people have even gone further to suggest that unlike traditional belief, emotional intelligence might bear more weight in determining one's success rather than the traditional intelligence quotient. This claim is really disruptive to what we have been raised to know all our lives. We can see that in school, the student with the highest GPA would be praised as an example of the model student we should emulate. At different levels of education, there are tests given to all the students, standard across the board regardless of the student's interests or abilities. And using these tests, we get to determine who are better students and have a higher chance for success in life by those who score higher with those who do not perform as well are assumed to have a less probability of success in life regardless of what their other talents may be. The culture created in all our education systems is centered on their cognitive mental abilities with regards to their intelligence quotient and not taking into account other factors that are fundamental to the wholesome growth of these students. So it is also a culture that has been institutionalized where we have to focus more on the IQ rather than the EQ. Some people have then gone to conduct studies and claim that EQ is more important to the success of a person than their IQ. We shall explore those claims later on in this chapter but let us first see why emotional intelligence is actually important.

It is a widespread consensus that soft skills have had a great role in determining our relations with other people in our lives and have led to what would be seemingly increased success at different tasks both in and out of the work place. This is largely as a result of how the people with these soft skills are doing their interactions with people. Habits such as actively listening to a person with intent not only to respond but also to give constructive feedback. Such skills would be very vital in the workplace where one's employees and subordinates will feel that they are greatly valued based on the attention you took in their queries and helping them deal with the bottlenecks they encounter. This feeling of involvement and appreciation created by these skills mastered by the leadership then lead to the employees having a greater commitment and dedication to the goals of their leaders and subsequently that of their organization. These focus on the members in their tasks plays a crucial role in their performance, output, and attitude and therefore highlighting the value that these soft skills developed with increased emotional intelligence have on success.

Increased emotional intelligence leads to an increased capacity of a person to develop their empathic abilities. There are able to put themselves in another person's shoes and see things from their perspective. By having this greater understanding of how exactly they feel and relate to a certain situation, these leaders are able to adjust accordingly to their employee's needs and demands, and this will, in turn, make the employees perform better as they know that their leadership has considered them in their goal setting. A Harvard Business review article suggested that most people in senior management were lacking regarding the level of empathy they had developed. Hence, creating a deeper understanding and vast knowledge of emotional intelligence would help in reducing that deficiency and in turn increasing our productivity.

Emotional intelligence that is mature in a person enables them to easily identify the emotions of the people they are around, and with that information, they are able to adjust their behaviors accordingly to best suit that situation. Using also this ability, they are able to influence the behavior and reactions of the opposite party in a manner that is advantageous to them. It also makes it easier for a person to recognize their own emotions and therefore they can control their reactions. The implications are far reaching, which helps them maintain their composure in the cases of a crisis and this would, in turn, reassure their members that the problem can be dealt with. Furthermore, being able to control their emotions would also help them in making better decisions and communicate more effectively with their team members making them better leaders.

Emotional intelligence is characterized by 4 main skills

1.Self-awareness – this is an innate ability for one to introspect and understand their emotions and how they will lead to them behaving in a certain manner in different scenarios.

2.Social awareness – This refers to a person's ability to observe and make sense of the emotions experienced by other people

3.Self-management – This refers to an individual's ability to use their self-awareness to adapt to their different situations and tailor their behavior accordingly.

4.Relationship management – This involves the use of the skills above and effectively and successfully manage the interactions between themselves and other people.

Our use of the soft skills that we have developed with our increased emotional intelligence then goes a long way in our interactions with other people. How we navigate, these relations are the things that will help us in increasing the trust other people have in us and how these relations are after that strengthened. The ability to be likable also enables people to let down their guards with us and honestly conversing with us making ourselves more approachable, a trait very vital to great leadership. The emotions that we give out to our team and those that we evoke from them are the indicators that distinguish mediocre leadership to an exemplary and effective one.

So why exactly is emotional intelligence important and which traits to they involve most? Firstly, compassion. Compassion is the ability of a person to be concerned with the emotions of other people. For leaders, this is an important trait to have as this enables them to embrace the emotions of their team members and identify with them. This translates to sending the subconscious message that the leadership and the organization as a whole care about them and their needs.

Secondly, increased emotional intelligence increases a person's effectiveness in communication. Being able to effectively communicate your goals and target of the organization would lead to better execution of tasks increasing the level of efficiency in time and productivity. If one is not able to communicate their vision effectively then it makes it harder for them to motivate their team members to the achievement of those goals. Effective communication also creates room for clear instruction to be given making it easier for the task at hand to be done with little to no room for error. Effective communication also goes beyond just issuing instructions but also in one's ability to listen attentively and through that read into the situation and emotions and responding appropriately to it.

Increased self-awareness of a leader is also instrumental for his emotional intelligence. With an increased level of self-understanding, he is fully aware as a leader of his strengths and weaknesses, and with that, he is able to use this to his advantages. He uses this knowledge in the recruiting of talent for the areas he may feel a tad less inadequate in. This self-awareness also helps a person easily recognize the strengths and weaknesses of the other people that they are working with and in this, tasks are able to be assigned to the ones who would perform them optimally. Without this self-understanding, it becomes less likely for a leader to be able to adequately motivate their team based on their abilities.

"Knowing others is knowledge; knowing yourself is genuine shrewdness. Acing others is quality; acing yourself is genuine power. If you understand that you have enough, you are really rich," - Lao Tzu. Knowing oneself and acting from that fact attracts individuals to a leader. Being genuine, settling on choices that are in arrangement with how a leader really works infrequently requires second-speculating. Such a leader must comprehend their own particular esteems and be reliable in applying them. As a major aspect of that, the leader needs to have the strength to maintain them, without dismissing reality

Furthermore, respect is not just about others; the sincerely smart leader hones a sense of pride. How a leader treats themselves matters, since it is reflected back in the general population, he or she oversees. A leader who regards themselves as well as other people doesn't talk impolitely whenever, notwithstanding when botches happen. The best approach to do get the best out of individuals is not through disparaging conduct, but rather by treating all individuals the same in each circumstance.

Leaders who have enthusiasm demonstrate their feelings and powerlessness, and they interface with numerous representatives on a passionate level, too. Many leaders are logical, however in the event that they are recently cool and figuring, there might be excessively separate amongst them and their subordinates to genuinely be in a similar group. Fascisms don't work in an organization, particularly as a long haul answer for representative engagement or faithfulness. Even though this doesn't mean a leader with heart is a sucker or endures improper conduct (or messy work) it is possible that it implies tending to a subordinate with warmth. Segregated unequivocal quality without sympathy is ruthless.

If a leader is not kidding constantly, at that point it makes an extremely grim condition. A few leaders are hesitant to be light since they need to be considered important. It's typically an indication of uncertainty. A candidly canny leader presents adjust. Individuals tend to work harder and more quick witted when there is a feeling of fun. Resolve is connected to profitability, and as a pioneer, this way to impart a positive vitality to the workspace.

As the head of the team, there will be an emergency and quiet circumstances when things are not advancing. Whatever size the business, it's essential to not fall into overpower or go overboard. Individuals seek the leader for prompts on the best way to react to the conditions, and if a leader is sure while dealing with issues, it will help keep the group feeling the same. Incredible authority is tied in with having the certainty to settle on choices and not the second figure them. Those who motivate others to take after into the obscure, do as such having fearlessness.

Instinctive leaders settle on snappy choices in light of a lifetime of amassed astuteness and comprehension. Driving a group through a new region, without a guide, means the world is indeterminate, and the higher the hazard, the higher the weight. A rationale is critical, however, can't be the main deciding variable for settling on a choice. A leader who believes his or her gut will take the fundamental measures that move others to do likewise.

Finally, in an investigation led by IBM, 200 CEO expressed: "The present business condition is unstable, unverifiable and progressively complicated. As a result, the capacity to make something that is both original and fitting is best of the brain." Not all choices are straightforward, it's tied in with having the capacity to veer off and look outside of the limits of construed creativity for an alternate choice. Collective conceptualizing without any holds banned can bring a fresh and inventive answer for a test. Advancement is the after effect of creativity. A leader who unhesitatingly advances differing imaginative thinking and creativity will touch base by taking great leaps that make developments.

Additionally, we possess both rational and emotional judgments. In huge part, our emotional quotient worked to increase our chances of survival. At the point when man initially meandered the earth, whenever he experienced new things he expected to settle on immediate arrangements about whether the experience included something he could eat or something that may attempt to eat him. Depending on the intelligence quotient, which works much slower than the emotional intelligence, may have implied the annihilation of humanity. The emotional rationale would, however, spring more vigorously into action warranting a quicker reaction by man. Be that as it may, unless we figure out how to control our emotional intelligence, we will settle on heaps of awful choices and unpleasant decisions.

And as we mentioned before, having a high EQ plays a vital role in increasing our chances of success in life. Below are some of how this can be achieved,

Emotional intelligence can contribute to a large extent impact one's success and longevity at a job more than IQ. How relatable you are with your colleagues and how you maneuver those social settings will contribute to how you fit into the company. Similarly, increased emotional intelligence helps one to understand what is at stake at the moment and by enabling them to delay gratification, they can lay the right foundations at the beginning of a task. This innate ability to wait on the rewards have been proven to be a trait present in more successful people. This type of mentality then translates to different aspects of their lives in their everyday choices such as what and the quantity of the things they are eating or the type of entertainment activities they involve themselves with.

Notwithstanding, higher levels of emotional intelligence also helps to better relations with other people. Our understanding and management of our emotional temperaments are vital in our relations with other people. We have to comprehend our emotions, where they originate from, and how to legitimately express them. We won't keep up sound relationships unless we can control our feelings, impart our emotions in a productive way, and comprehend the sentiments of the other people you are interacting with.

Also, there is an immediate association between our emotional well-being and our physical well-being. On the off chance that our lives are loaded with stressful situations, our physical well-being endures. It has been evaluated that well more than 80% of our medical issues are stress related. We encounter stress principally because we are not happy inwardly and not at peace emotionally. We have to comprehend the connection between our emotional welfare and our physical well-being.

Sadly, there's an immediate association between poor emotional intelligence and the rising rate of crime being conducted. Youngsters who have poor emotional aptitudes end up plainly as social outsiders at an extremely young age. This may result in them turning into bullies due to their lack of control of their emotions and rage. They may have figured out how to respond with clenched hands as opposed to being open to dialogue and reason. Poor social and emotional abilities add to poor performance in their class setting and additionally sentiments of dissatisfaction. Regarding their school work, these students lag behind, and it is highly likely that they would associate themselves with students in the same predicament. Their way to involvement in criminal activities begins at a very young age. It cannot be ignored that their upbringing and home setting is a big contributor to this, it is not uncommon that they are subjected to this as a result of their poor emotional intelligence.

Chapter 3: Ways Through Which One Can Gain Emotional Intelligence

An ideal approach to enhancing and improving your emotional intelligence is through training oneself in their everyday living. Through training and getting input on your execution, ideally by an accomplished emotional intelligence coach or trainer, you can alter your conduct and turn out to be more successful in perceiving and dealing with your own feelings and additionally the feelings of others.

Everybody has parts of their lives that they can better. Here are some ways that you can take a shot at improving your emotional intelligence with the goal that you can start to have any difference in the various circumstances you might find yourself in. Albeit each of the aptitudes can benefit you somehow, you may discover a few abilities more critical than others, contingent upon your present circumstance.

First, self-awareness is a paramount aspect of emotional intelligence. From numerous points of view, this territory is the foundation from which all other aspects of emotional intelligence stem off. Keeping in mind the end goal of effectively reading and interpreting other people's feelings from how they behave, what they say and how they say it, for instance, it should be the first order of business for you to know and effectively understand your feelings.

You can turn out to be more mindful of your feelings through different types of reflection and meditation. By participation in a course, joining a gathering of people with similar interests, or contracting a trainer, you can utilize these strategic procedures to end up noticeably more mindful of your body, your emotions, and your considerations.

You can likewise turn out to be more mindful by utilizing your journal to record your sentiments and behaviors at different predetermined time interims. By expanding the vocabulary used in describing your emotional states and utilizing this knowledge to in turn express your full scope of sentiments all through different parts of the day, you can make sense of how to give more careful consideration to your feelings. Notwithstanding expressing your feelings, focus on their intensity. Rate your feelings from 1 to 10. The better you can measure your feelings, the all the more effectively you can predict them and adjust your behavior in a more suitable manner.

Similarly, learning on how best to express your feelings can regularly help you in dealing with those feelings. You can, obviously, suppress everything and not share your genuine musings, sentiments, or convictions with anybody. Be that as it may, not exclusively is this approach hard to do, it makes for a desolate life. No one truly becomes more acquainted with you, and you don't become more acquainted with others exceptionally well, either. All people share the longing to have intimate and meaningful associations with a couple of individuals they consider trustworthy.

Then again, you can blabber out your deepest considerations, emotions, and convictions to everybody. This approach can likewise be a mix-up. As a matter of first importance, a few people don't think about your thoughts and sentiments. Second, others people may be irritated or offended by your divulgences or discover them inconsiderate. Go for a center ground, called confidence. Confidence is the fitting sharing of contemplations, emotions, and convictions. Fundamentally, you have to tell the correct individuals, at the perfect time, where it is that you stand on different subject matters.

Everybody has a tendency to approach their work every day doing what they need to do. However, what a number of individuals are truly amped up and excited for the work that they do? Many individuals feel that they're trapped in a hopeless cycle at their occupations. Be that as it may, somebody didn't forcibly cull them up and put them where they are. Typically, by pursuing opportunities to make more money, individuals wind up stuck working at where they are currently working.

Scarcely any individuals endeavor to do the sort of work that truly energizes them. Many people have an enthusiasm for some work, hobbies, or interests somewhere inside, yet you can't effectively discover it. You may know some starving craftsmen who avoid general employment with expectations of making their fantasies and dreams materialize. You will most likely be unable to effortlessly look for some employment that you're enthusiastic about, yet with the effective planning, one can achieve this dream.

A few people assume that they're great at everything while there are others continually think little of their qualities and underestimate them. In a utopian situation, obviously, one should be able to precisely know your abilities and shortcomings. Knowing oneself encourages you to settle in on some life decisions. For instance, by concentrating on your strengths, you can get a greater amount of what you need out of life. Seeking after the things you're great at and have an enthusiasm for —, for example, science, music, workmanship, composing, open talking, carpentry, or cultivating — empowers you to carry on with a wealthier and more full life. By concentrating on the various aspects of one's weaknesses, unless they meddle with your life, you are more inclined to keep yourself away from getting the most out of life. When you need to make decisions, you may get messages that appear to originate from your gut. Certain decisions can rest easy, and others may give you a nauseous feeling. You may think about these emotions as signals from your heart of what it truly wants, instead of from your head. Individuals are regularly guided by their emotions, which they may not be completely mindful of.

Compassion and empathy are to a great degree very strong feelings. The best lawmakers, philanthropic givers, media identities and moguls such as Oprah Winfrey, and many other business leaders are highly empathetic. Expanding your capacity to understand what other people may be going through enables you to get nearer to others and connect with them at a level where you understand each other as well as garner their support for occasions where you may you require it, and defuse conceivably high-charged circumstances. By demonstrating to other people that you truly comprehend what kind of emotions he harbors, you pick up a specific level of regard. You illustrate, for instance, that you're not egotistical. Begin by being more empathic by giving careful consideration to other individuals. Listen precisely when speaking with somebody. Tune into both what she lets you know and what she needs you to listen. By showing signs of improvement at grabbing and focusing on what individuals are truly attempting to state, you turn out to be more empathic.

On the off chance that you can deal with the feelings of individuals around you, you have a great talent. You've most likely observed leaders who can quiet down or console an irate group. Then again, you've most likely additionally perceived how a few people can bungle the feelings of others. Ponder on the number of times an insufficiently prepared CEO of an organization needed to confront the media in a period of crisis. By portraying the wrong nonverbal communication cues, use of the wrong tone of voice in his speech, or dodging answers to questions, these leaders made their audiences more irritated.

Overseeing other individuals' feelings is a two-stage activity. Simply take after these phases:

Work to increase your empathic ability. You have to place yourself in the other individual's shoes and feel his agony, delight, expectations, or fears. One path is by making personalized inquiries of individuals. Infer what you can by asking and watching their behavior. Does he like games or exercise? What are his most loved teams and hobbies? What is her favorite dessert? What brings her joy or sadness?

React to him in the way that you would need somebody to react to you to ease that agony. Handling another person's emotions requires a specific measure of ability. To start with, you have to know where you need to lead the other individual. Would you like to make somebody elated, quiet, watchful, or mindful, for instance? After you choose how you need her to feel, at that point you need to know how to take her to that mental space. Think about the last time that you heard a motivational speaker or watched a movie that truly impacted you. Impactful encounters more often than not include a buildup in which the speaker or director sets the mood for where he or she needs you to go inwardly. You can make this build up yourself by defining an objective or telling the individual where you need to go.

A few cases are

We need to take a gander at this circumstance tranquility.

As a family, we should know about what's happening.

Some terrible things have happened, and we must be vigil.

At that point, you can construct your case through stories or illustrations. You have to pass on the message to the next individual that you're both on a similar side — and it's advantageous to the two of you to be in agreement. By being predictable in your body act, your voice, and your message, you can convey a strong message that can move the other individual's feelings nearer to where you need them.

Furthermore, a social obligation is one of the most abnormal amounts of enthusiastic experience. It shows that you truly think about others, particularly those less blessed. Being socially mindful isn't about individual pick up — it's about what you can add to enable other to individuals.

Social duty has a few layers:

At a more fundamental level, you can give cash to philanthropy or a noble purpose. In spite of the fact that you need to give donations as part of any socially capable arrangement, gifts are just an initial phase all the while.

At the following level, you may enable a commendable association to gather cash. You can request from companions, relatives, neighbors, or individuals you work with. You can get included in occasions that raise cash — altruistic runs, auto washes, walkathons, or biking occasions.

The best parts of social obligation include you expressly adding to a worthy cause. Think about some ways that you can help other people who may require it. You might need to begin by distinguishing the causes that you see as most imperative to you. You may feel energetic about domestic violence, vagrancy, nourishment covers, elderly care, hospitalized individuals, particular ailments, particular causes, et cetera. After you decide on the cause that you need to help, consider how you can best contribute. You can serve on the board, be a charitable worker, or take an interest in any of various ways. Contact the office or association related with that reason and ask how you can offer assistance.

Dealing with your feelings, particularly being impulsive, gives another mainstay of EQ (notwithstanding monitoring your feelings and overseeing other individuals' feelings). By winding up plainly more sincerely mindful, you better set yourself up for emotional self-administration. You can deal with your motivations in three fundamental ways:

Diversion: When you sense an issue in drive control going ahead, you can most rapidly manage it by diverting yourself. Move your reasoning by checking to ten or concentrating on arranged diverting contemplations. You can prepare yourself to rapidly change your contemplations, or the subject if in a discussion, to something, for example, the climate, where you intend to visit next month, a venture you're dealing with, or whatever other occasions are.

Explanatory: A logical approach includes halting and investigating your contemplations when you feel indiscreet. You can make inquiries, for example,

Why am I pondering this upsetting issue or occasion?

By what means can suppose about this upsetting issue or occasion help me?

Might I be able to be considering something else?

What's a superior option thought?

Adapting: An adapting system includes various particular adapting musings that you hone ahead of time. These considerations incorporate proclamations, for example,

I know I can control my contemplations.

I can simply back off a bit.

Give me a chance to thoroughly consider this.

I don't need to surge with a reaction.

I can consider choices.

Procedures, for example, the ones in the first rundown can help you effectively manage upsetting issues or occasions when you hone them ahead of time. You can't successfully experiment with these methodologies on the fly. With arranging and practice, you can go far in managing imprudent considerations, words, and activities. Everybody has their schedules and methodology when it comes to getting things done. For a general public to run productively, it needs a specific measure of principles and controls. Be that as it may, you can encounter issues when you stall out stuck and wind up plainly unbendable to change. By being excessively inflexible you pass up a great opportunity for circumstances, fall behind in adapting new systems and methodologies, and tend to manage individual and work issues in the same, once in a while ineffective, ways.

Having high emotional intelligence includes knowing when to stick to and when to abandon your emotional attachments. At the point when it's a great opportunity to proceed onward, individuals high in EQ can make that modification.

If you discover change troublesome, take a gander at the conceivable outcomes. What may happen if you remain with the present state of affairs? Then again, where may you be if you take the path of least resistance? Change is a piece of development. All through life, new encounters, and new open doors can give you individual and expert satisfaction, and you should be interested in these progressions. Despite the fact that you may think that it's awkward to attempt new things, a great many people locate the fleeting pains worth the long haul pick up. Some portion of developing as a man includes adopting new abilities and approaches and encountering new connections and places.

How glad would you say you are? No, truly, how cheerful would you say you are, in a size of 1 to 10? Is it true that you are a 5 or a 7? What about a 9? Individuals with relatively higher emotional intelligence are jolly individuals. What's more, they're not quite recently cheerful because great things transpire to their favor. Bliss (genuine satisfaction, which feels like a warm, consistent gleam inside your body), originates from the back to front. A man who deals with this feeling admirably awakens cheerful in the morning. What's more, when he experiences challenges for the duration of the day, he can keep up a specific level of his bliss. Truth be told, his bliss floats his spirits while experiencing the hardships of everyday living, and it keeps his mind clear, keeping him from becoming involved with ineffective self-centeredness or other non-accommodating feelings. Cheerful individuals concocted a larger number of answers for issues than miserable or discouraged individuals do.

Albeit sad individuals, for the most part, give careful consideration to points of interest than glad individuals, cheerful individuals fulfill more than dismal individuals. Obviously, because bliss and misery are feelings, they do vacillate. In this way, you can control your state of mind to fill your own particular need. Being candidly astute includes knowing when to be cheerful, miserable, energized, on edge, or even watchful.

Individuals favor being around other individuals who are high in spirit and happy. Glad leaders have supporters who are exceptionally locked in. You can discover many focal points to being glad. Individuals will welcome you more, you can traverse intense circumstances less demanding, you can rest easy, and you'll be more useful to others. Research even demonstrates that cheerful individuals live more (or despairing individuals bite the dust sooner).

Not very many individuals truly know how to deal with their satisfaction. Individuals very frequently connect happiness with material things or with getting things from others. The truly happy individuals are the those who would rather give to people than receive things from them. The general population who spread joy have a tendency to be more joyful themselves.

Ideally, while you work to increase your capacity of emotional intelligence, you recall that it costs you nothing to spread bliss, and what you get consequently is extremely valuable.

Chapter 4: Learning How to Control One's Emotions

Emotions that we experience in our lives can tend to be the biggest motivators or distractors to a lot of the things that we do in our lives. Every day, we make decisions on things to do or not to do based on how we feel. What we feel, more often than not, will dictate how we think, what we say and what we get to do either for ourselves or the people around us. Being as it may, it is paramount that we have control of our emotions or otherwise have to suffer the pains of regretting decisions and actions that we did. Being on either end of our emotional state is not ideal for any person, therefore, they should take up their emotions with a grain of salt, try and maintain a balance to help them live life optimally. So how can someone harness the skill of maintaining their emotions? These are a few practical steps a person can adopt to maintain their emotions.

Avoid the urge to react immediately. Responding instantly to your emotions can be a gross error. It is ensured that you'll say or perform a task that you'll later lament. Before annulling the trigger with your emotional logic, take a full breath and balance out your inner emotions. Keep on breathing deeply for some minutes, feeling as your muscles relax and your heart rate comes back to ordinary. As you wind up noticeably more settled, insist to yourself that is only a temporary situation.

Get a healthy out for these emotions. Seeing as you learned on how to manage these emotions, it is imperative for you to learn how to rid yourself of those emotions in a manner that is beneficial and sustainable. Bottling up of emotions is detrimental to someone's health, and therefore one can employ the services of a psychiatrist to speak about your emotions with or find a friend you can trust and do the same. Some people also opt to use sport and working out as an outlet for themselves and their emotions. There are many ways to release these emotions from within ourselves, therefore, one should work to identify that which best suits them.

Never lose sight of the end goal. Often, strong emotions warrant strong and immediate responses from us, however; we should always try to see the bigger picture. Understand that whatever happens to us happens for a particular reason, and we should try and understand what this reason might be and how it may, in turn, be beneficial to us and our journey. In the same manner, it is also fundamental for a person to take charge of the thoughts that they have. What we entertain as our thoughts often dictate our emotions and how we react to different situations. Therefore, if we maintain a positive train of thought, our emotions will also be of the pleasant nature benefiting not only ourselves but those around us too.

Identify what we could consider your emotional triggers and forgive them. This is in a bid to dissociate yourself with them and be free and full control of your emotions. Emotional triggers could be things, places or people who are able to make you feel a certain way .it could be anything from anger to regret or even insecurities. Therefore, when one learns to forgive them, they consequently dissociate themselves with them and gain back control of their own emotions.

Emotions are part of our day to day lives but the manner in which we respond our emotional bursts implicate our lifestyle. With this regard, one should put a conscious effort into controlling their emotions to live a more fulfilled life.

Chapter 5: Emotional Intelligence and Others

For one to be able to effectively manage their emotional intelligence and their relationships with other people, one must nurture their empathic ability and develop their empathy. Empathy is considered as one's ability to put themselves in the shoes of another and feel what they are feeling and understand what they are going through. This trait is fundamental to a person who intends to develop their emotional intelligence and broaden their capacity. So what are some of how a person can develop their empathy and foster better relations with other people?

Develop a curiosity about strangers. Talking to people that come from outside of our normal circles puts us in a unique position. We get to hear more about the lives that other people are leading and therefore we get to experience new emotions through their speech, and this also puts us in the unique position of getting to read into the emotions of people who we would regularly not be in contact with. This is why people with high empathic abilities are curious about strangers and want to interact with people they have not interacted with before.

Another way that one can develop their empathy is by listening attentively to people as they speak and share their experiences and allowing themselves to be vulnerable. By listening attentively to other people, highly empathic people can fully immerse themselves in the exact emotions of the person they are listening to and fathom their needs in that state. Listening with intent is not the end of it. One should be able to make themselves vulnerable enough and open up themselves to the other person and by being vulnerable one can connect deeper with people.

Last but not least, one should work to try and empathize with people who would naturally not get their sympathy. It is easy to empathize with people you are familiar with, or people who would naturally be considered vulnerable with children but trying to expand this circle to people who have different beliefs and opinions to our own would work wonders in honing our empathic abilities more and consequently increase our emotional intelligence.

Conclusion

Thank for enduring to the finish of the book. I hope it was a delightful experience reading it. Give us a chance to trust it was instructive and ready to furnish you with the right techniques, which will help you to accomplish your objectives, whatever it is that they might be. Because you've completed this book doesn't mean there is nothing left to learn on the theme, extending your points of view is the best way to discover the dominance you look for

The next step is to stop reading and to get starting doing whatever it is that was described herein that would propel you to the next level of success that your increased understanding on the topic has afforded you. If you find it a little difficult to actualize whatever you have learned in this book, it would be my recommendation for you to identify an accountability partner that would help you in consciously affecting the things you have learned and in due course of time, you will become more accustomed than you ever expected.

When you have completed your underlying preparations, it is important to comprehend that they are only the first stage of planning. Your best shots for general achievement will drop by setting aside the opportunity to learn whatever number essential abilities as could reasonably be expected. Just by utilizing your informed status as a launch pad to a better state of preparation will you have the capacity to genuinely rest soundly realizing that you are set up for everything without exception that life chooses to toss at you.

Finally, if you found this book useful in any way, a review on Amazon is always appreciated!

Description

If you were browsing the shelves of bookstores around you or scoured the ends of the internet for an all in one resource point on emotional intelligence, I am pleased to tell you that your search has ended. We had recognized the need for more emphasis to be given to emotional intelligence. We then made it our mission to equip people with the necessary information required to enable them to be more informed on the subject matter prompting behavior change with regards to EQ.

This information goes a long way in causing a paradigm shift in our mentality, and it would shed more light on aspects of our life that we have not paid much mind to. This type of information would consequently be instrumental in improving our quality of life and in better nurturing future generations to live life optimally with increased emotional intelligence.

Do not resign to a fate of being unaware of the subject matter but arm yourself with information that will help you successfully navigate through life. With that said, I encourage you to start today by purchasing this book! I promise it is going to be worth it.